How To Meditate God's Word

by
Dennis Burke

HARRISON HOUSE
Tulsa, Oklahoma

8th Printing

How To Meditate God's Word
ISBN 0-89274-241-0
Copyright © 1982 by Dennis Burke
P. O. Box 793
Arlington, Texas 76010

Published by Harrison House, Inc.
P. O. Box 35035
Tulsa, Oklahoma 74153

Contents

1
What It Means
To Meditate

There is a great difference between fact and truth. The truth in God's Word is more than just fact.

A theological fact will remain totally unassociated and detached from a person's life. Truth, however, is alive, creative, and life-changing.

When a person begins to allow the Word of God to mold his thoughts and activities, he will start moving out of a life of theological fact and into a warm, spiritual, life-giving understanding of truth.

Meditation in the Word of God is one of the greatest keys to obtaining understanding and truth.

Some Eastern religions teach that meditation is allowing your mind to become completely blank and empty, but that is far from the truth. To meditate is to fill your thoughts with the thoughts of God, to be consumed with the things God has said. When you become consumed with what He has said, it becomes effortless to do the things He said to do.

The Psalmist David said it this way:

I have more understanding than all my teachers: for thy testimonies are my meditation (Ps. 119:99).

The entrance of thy words giveth light; it giveth understanding unto the simple (Ps. 119:130).

Meditation is not intended merely to produce more knowledge, but also to give an understanding of God, of His ways and His Word.

When you begin to meditate the Word of God, you will have illumination and the understanding of how to walk in what God is revealing to you.

Joshua 1:8 is a classic scripture on meditation:

This book of the law shall not depart out of thy mouth; but thou shalt meditate therein day and night, that thou mayest observe to do according to all that is written therein: for then thou shalt make thy way prosperous, and then thou shalt have good success.

One purpose of meditation is to place you in a position of "doing" God's Word. Joshua said meditation day and night will cause you to "observe to do" all that is written. You must observe before you can do. You will see into the Word and revelation knowledge will come, enabling you to act according to what you have seen. True meditation will bring you to the place of responding to God's Word with action. Faith demands action.

The results of meditating day and night are wonderful! Joshua 1:8 says, *. . . for then thou shalt make thy way prosperous, and then thou shalt have good success.*

Notice God said, **Thou** *shalt make thy way prosperous.* God is not going to make your way prosperous. You make your way prosperous. God cannot do the Word for you. No one else can do it for you. But once you become a doer of God's Word, you will begin to prosper for yourself.

God has already released His power in order for you to live a life of prosperity and success. His success is available *now*.

This verse in Joshua is the only place in the *King James Version* of the Bible that records the word *success.* God is linking your success together with your commitment to His Word. If you will meditate in His Word and be a doer of the Word, success is inevitable.

Notice 1 Timothy 4:15 which says, *Meditate upon these things; give thyself wholly to them; that thy profiting may appear to all.*

As the Word of God takes preeminence in your life, you will profit. You will increase. You will become more productive.

God wants the world to see what He has done in you. He wants your success and stability to appear to all those with whom you come into contact. He wants your progress to become evident to all those around you. You will become a living example of the true nature of God. He is a loving God and a giving Father. Just as Jesus was "the radiance of His glory and the exact representation of His nature," we are to be like Him. (Heb. 1:3, NASB.)

Give yourself completely over to what God has said. Become totally engrossed in His commandments. Commit yourself to them.

Some have experienced the most frustrating time of their lives by earnestly desiring the results the Word will produce, but neglecting to do what the Word instructs.

Hearing the fact that you have rights as a believer is an exciting message. However, without meditating in the Word of God — observing to do all that is written therein — you will never enjoy the privileges that are rightfully yours. No one receives the results of faith without the commitment to live by faith. Only committed, diligent people receive rewards. (Heb. 11:6.)

When you give yourself wholly to meditation in God's Word, God becomes the guarantee of your profit! God is getting actively involved with your life. When you wholly commit to God, He wholly commits to you.

Blessed is the man that walketh not in the counsel of the ungodly, nor standeth in the way of sinners, nor sitteth in the seat of the scornful.

But his delight is in the law of the Lord; and in his law doth he meditate day and night.

And he shall be like a tree planted by the rivers of water, that bringeth forth his fruit in his season; his leaf also shall not wither; and whatsoever he doeth shall prosper.

Psalm 1:1-3

Once again, here are instructions to meditate day and night. The person who will follow these instructions will prosper in everything he does. The person who meditates on God's Word day and night becomes overtaken by God's blessings. He becomes a success at whatever he sets his hand to do. He is linked to his life Source, so that his leaf does not wither or fade, even in times of drought.

When God's Word is your delight, you are immovable. You are like a tree planted firmly. You will become a source of strength to those in need. That is true prosperity.

2
How To Meditate
God's Word

In Joshua 1:8 and Psalm 1:1-3 God
said that we are to meditate day and
night. How is that done? Many times
people have had the idea that
meditation must be reading their
Bibles. There are people who have quit
their jobs so they could stay home to
read their Bibles, but it has only
resulted in failure. God's Word says,
. . . *if any would not work, neither
should he eat* (2 Thess. 3:10); and, *If any
provide not for his own, he . . . is worse
than an infidel* (1 Tim. 5:8).

It is not possible to read your Bible
day and night. Even if you could make it
through one twenty-four-hour day, that

would be all you could handle. No one can continue reading day and night and expect to get anything else done in his life.

To live by faith does not mean "quit your job." If a person is not successful in living by faith *with* a job, then he will never be successful in living by faith *without* a job.

God is aware of the fact that we have personal responsibilities, yet He has still instructed us to meditate day and night. Does this mean that God is unconcerned about our personal responsibilities? Is this commandment so unreasonable? No!

There are various avenues in which to meditate the Word of God. In this chapter we will discuss some of these avenues. As we do, I want you to keep in mind that meditation is not just reading your Bible. However, in order to meditate, you must have a time of study and reading. Everything you meditate must originate from the Word of God.

Three Ways To Meditate

1. Mutter God's Word

Remember, Joshua 1:8 says, *This book of the law shall not depart out of thy mouth.* This does not mean you are to keep the Word in your mouth, but rather you are to speak it out your mouth. It should not be away from your lips at any time. Continually speak it.

Everyone knows how to mutter. To mutter means to speak things quietly or under your breath, speaking to yourself, regardless of whether people are present to hear you. You may mutter while you are driving your car, or maybe while you are shopping.

Have you ever lost something and asked yourself, "Now where did I leave it? Where was the last place I remember seeing it?"

This is muttering to yourself. It is actually one of the definitions given for meditation. You can use muttering as a means to meditate God's Word. During your study time take one or two of the scriptures promised to you and mutter them to yourself during the day, keeping them fresh within you and allowing them to saturate you and wash through you.

Romans 10:8 says, *The word is nigh thee, even in thy mouth, and in thy heart.* Jesus said, . . . *for out of the abundance of the heart the mouth speaketh* (Matt. 12:34).

There is power in the Word of God, and you need that power working in you and affecting your entire life. Mutter to yourself like this:

"My God shall supply all my needs according to His riches in glory. God meets my needs, not according to *my need,* but according to *His riches.* That is abundance.

"Jesus, You said that You came that I might have life and have it more abundantly. You are the great El Shaddai, the God Who is more than enough to meet my every need."

That is meditating on God's provision, based on what He has already promised. This will begin to affect your outlook. You are meditating on God's abundant supply and on the fact that you are a child that your heavenly Father provides for.

It is easy to see how you can meditate in this fashion anytime and anyplace. At the office when important decisions are necessary, you can mutter to yourself, "Jesus has been made unto me wisdom. I have the wisdom of God available to me. In Christ are hid all the treasures of wisdom and knowledge and He dwells in me. The Holy Spirit will reveal the answer to me." By doing this, you put yourself in position to make your way prosperous and have good success.

Psalm 63:5,6 says, *My soul shall be satisfied as with marrow and fatness; and my mouth shall praise thee with joyful lips: when I remember thee upon my bed, and meditate on thee in the night watches.*

When you remember who this God is that lives inside you, you are, in fact, meditating on Him. He is a faithful God; He will be faithful to you when you walk in His Word. He is a merciful God; His mercy endures forever. He is a God of abundance; He has given all that He has to you.

Meditation on Him will bring your mind and emotions under control. Your soul will become satisfied as you mutter to yourself of the abundance of God.

This is the most powerful tool to use to keep control of your mind. Many times your mind will begin to waver. You will question whether you are going to make it through this problem. But if you will meditate and mutter on who God is and what He has promised you, your mind will have to be quiet long enough to hear what your mouth is saying.

The Word of God coming out your mouth will change your attitude toward the situation. You will begin to take on the renewed mind of Christ. You will begin to think in line with God's thoughts of possibility, not your ideas of failure.

2. Speak Aloud

It is interesting to note that the Hebrew word in Joshua 1:8 translated *meditate* is rendered "to speak" in the following verses:

For my mouth shall speak (or meditate) *truth* (Prov. 8:7).

And my tongue shall speak (or meditate) *of thy righteousness and of thy praise all the day long* (Ps. 35:28).

The mouth of the righteous speaketh (meditate) *wisdom, and his tongue talketh of judgment* (Ps. 37:30).

When you are speaking to others of the great God you serve, the wonderful things He has done, and the immense wisdom He possesses, you are actually involved in meditation. It is beneficial for you to hear how God has moved on behalf of another person. You can witness, before your eyes, someone who has received God's miracle power; and if God will do it for someone else, He will do it for you. Speak God's Word to one another. Talk of His faithfulness.

Ephesians 5:19 expresses it this way: *Speaking to yourselves in psalms and hymns and spiritual songs, singing and making melody in your heart to the Lord.*

Speaking to one another will cause your whole man to be edified. This is building up one another in the Word of God. Fellowship is so vitally important among believers. People need to hear of the wondrous works of God. They need to hear that God is still a miracle-working God. The world needs to hear that God is still in the healing business. *And they overcame him by the blood of the Lamb, and by the word of their testimony* (Rev. 12:11).

Never allow shyness or timidity to hold you back. Refuse to be dominated by a spirit of fear.

I will meditate also of all thy work, and talk of thy doings.

Psalm 77:12

Talking of God's doings is meditating His Word. **Meditation and the words you speak are directly linked.** Whatever is in your heart in abundance will come out your mouth.

Worry is a form of meditation. However, it is not meditating on what God says; it is meditating on what the news says, or what people say, or what could happen.

Speaking the Word does not mean that you only speak in chapter and verse. But it does mean that what you speak is uplifting, edifying, and in line with what God has said.

When you hear the wisdom of God and truth coming from your own lips, it not only builds up others, but it edifies you as well. You will believe what you say before you will believe what anyone else has to say.

Words that spring up from your spirit and are spoken out your mouth flood your entire being as you speak them. **You** are building and recharging **yourself** as you speak.

Faith cometh by hearing, and hearing by the word of God.
Romans 10:17

You will hear and receive as you speak the Word of God from your own mouth.

3. Muse

To muse means to "ponder, consider, and study closely." This is the aspect of meditation that most people are aware of: taking hold of a promise or a truth and going over it again and again; not going over it in order to memorize it, but *squeezing* out all the richness; thinking on it and allowing it to wash through your inner man.

The most vivid illustration I can give of musing is a cow chewing her cud. A cow grazes through the pasture, finds an abundance of tasty grass, chews it, and finally swallows it. Later, up comes the chewed grass to chew again. Each time the cow brings up the old cud and chews it, she is refining it and making it more and more a part of her system. She chews all the nutrients out of it; the stems and stalk are removed until it is consumed into her body.

This is the most descriptive, powerful example of meditation. Treat the Word of God just as a cow chews her cud. Feed on a scripture over and over again, swallow it, then bring it back up again, going over it again and again. Each time you chew on it, you are demanding all the nutrients out of it, making it more and more a part of your being.

This is the meat of meditation. Bible reading is like the potatoes in your spiritual diet. You must have meat in your diet to remain healthy. The meat comes as you chew on a promise. Let it circulate through you. Squeeze the life of God from it. Let the power of God and the revelation of that promise become a reality to you. God will show you wonderful things because you have given your interest to the Word.

In regard to a particular scripture, ask yourself, "How does this golden nugget of truth work for me? How can this apply to my life?"

This will bring the greatest discovery of revelation knowledge you have ever known. As you meditate, you will receive fresh revelation for yourself. There is no substitute for knowing you have heard from the Holy Spirit. There is no replacement for time spent in meditation and fellowship with God.

He will become intimate with you. This is the desire of God: to have an intimate relationship with His children. The Apostle James said, *Draw nigh to God, and he will draw nigh to you* (James 4:8).

3
Spiritual Imagination

There lies within every person the ability to imagine. The human imagination is a powerful force. The inbred creativity of God flows from your spirit into your imagination.

Many great ideas have been born into the world because a believer used his imagination. On the other hand, perverse and corrupt things have happened as a result of a corrupt imagination. The unregenerated man has powerful potential through the use of the imagination. Problems arise when the source of ideas is not based on the thoughts of God.

In Genesis 11:6 you can see the capabilities man has with his imagination outside of God: *. . . and now nothing will be restrained from them, which they have imagined to do.*

Just think of what is available to the person, born of the Spirit of God, who would allow the Holy Spirit to form his imaginations. The possibilities are limitless! This is where creative ability begins for the believer. You are capable of getting an inner picture of the Word of God working on your behalf. See yourself living in the fulfillment of the promises of God.

In your time of meditation, set aside a time to use the creative ability God has given you. Imagine yourself doing what the Word says. See Jesus healing the sick through you. See yourself laying hands on the sick, and the sick recovering. Imagine yourself living within the abundance of God, having all sufficiency and able to give unto every good work. See yourself healed in your physical body.

Of course, the Bible says to cast down *imaginations, and every high thing that exalteth itself against the knowledge of God, and bringing into captivity every thought to the obedience of Christ* (2 Cor. 10:5). This scripture expounds the point I have already made. You are to use your spiritual imagination to exalt the knowledge of God and cause your thoughts to become obedient to Christ. In other words, you begin to see things the way Christ sees them.

As a believer, you probably don't have trouble seeing yourself enjoying heaven in the ages to come. You may have heard people talk about heaven and visualized for yourself what the Bible says about it. Most of us have some idea of what heaven will be like and can easily picture ourselves in that setting. Faith has come, in that particular area, because of what we have heard.

Using that same principle you can begin to imagine yourself enjoying what God has said about you in this age. Begin to picture yourself in the setting of God's desire for your life. He wants your body well and whole, free from pain. He wants your family to be united in harmony. He is eager to see your financial standing on the rise. He longs for your mind to be at peace, free from depression. His desire is for you to have success in every area of your life.

Who said you must live your life and never enjoy having more than enough? Who said your business would never make it? Who said your ministry would be ineffective? You don't find God saying those things! These are the type of imaginations we are to cast down.

There will always be people who will give you every reason why you can't enjoy God's best. If you dwell on these limitations, allowing them to mold your imaginations, then you can't make it!

Have you ever noticed that when you read a newspaper or hear a news broadcast telling of shortages or economic changes, your mind begins to picture the many varied effects these changes will have on you? Your mind receives these bits of information, then forms pictures based on that information.

This type of imagining is more widely known as worry. Worry is based on meditating on the will of the Devil. Have you ever worried about something wonderful happening to you? No! People worry about tragedy and calamity. Worry is meditating on the horrible things that *could* happen. It is so easy to imagine terrible things happening because of the negative course the world is following.

Think of the potential of a person who regularly feeds himself on the information supplied in God's Word. He could begin to visualize the Word producing fruit through him. The power of God would back him. The things which he imagines to do, based upon the promises of God, would not be withheld from him.

4

Guarding Your Heart

Pictures and images are formed in your spirit by what you continually hear and see. It is of the utmost importance that you use the Word of God to paint the pictures in your heart. This is the primary reason for the instructions in Proverbs 4:20,21:

My son, attend to my words; incline thine ear unto my sayings.

Let them not depart from thine eyes; keep them in the midst of thine heart.

Surround yourself with the Word of God. Let it saturate your entire being. God's Word is His integrity. He means exactly what He says. He has said you are righteous in His sight. Imagine yourself standing in His presence with confidence. He has said you are an able minister of the New Covenant. Get the picture clear in your heart of people responding to the Good News of Jesus as you minister to them.

Three things are mentioned in this scripture to show us how to attend to the Word.

1. *Incline thine ear unto my sayings.*

What a person hears will affect the way he sees things. If you listen to some religious tradition that says, "God will heal sometimes, but He doesn't heal everyone," that will affect how you view God's Word on healing. But when you continually hear, "Jesus healed them all," you can rest assured that healing is for you.

Jesus said it this way: *Take heed what ye hear: with what measure ye mete, it shall be measured to you: and unto you that hear shall more be given* (Mark 4:24).

The way you measure out the Word of God in your own life is the way success in the Word will be measured to you. When you put 100 percent into the Word, you will get 100 percent results. Likewise, if you put 60 percent into the Word, you will get 60 percent results. If you put 30 percent into the Word, you will get 30 percent results. Choose the measure of results you desire, then get into the Word accordingly.

The people who are truly hearing the Word are doing what God has said, and Jesus said that those who hear would receive more. Once you hear the Word and act on it, you receive more revelation knowledge from the Lord.

2. *Let them* (God's words) *not depart from thine eyes.*

This does not mean reading your Bible twenty-four hours a day. That would be impossible and very impractical. But you can look into the Bible,

see what God said He would do, and
then view what is happening around
you in the light of His Word.

In Luke 11:34 Jesus said, *The light of
the body is the eye: therefore when
thine eye is single, thy whole body also
is full of light.* To keep your body in the
light, you have to keep your eyes full of
light. The Word of God is light. Learn to
see with the eyes of your spirit. Seeing
things in line with God's Word will help
you keep your body and the circum-
stances around you in line with the
Word.

A powerful example of this
principle is found in Genesis 13:14,15.

*And the Lord said unto Abram,
after that Lot was separated from him,
Lift up now thine eyes, and look from
the place where thou art northward,
and southward, and eastward, and
westward:*

For all the land which thou seest, to thee will I give it, and to thy seed for ever.

Abram had to **see** the land. God said, *Lift up now thine eyes.* You must lift your spiritual eyes to "see" what God sees. God said that if Abram would see it, He would give him the land.

If you can see it, you can have it. If you can see health in your body, you can have it. If you can see prosperity in your life, you can have it. Whatever you can truly imagine on the inside can become a reality on the outside. If you cannot see it on the inside, you are hindered from ever experiencing it on the outside.

Abram had to see the land before he could have it. If he had only looked to the south, he would have received everything to the south. If you look into the Word and see everlasting life in heaven, you will only enjoy that portion of God's provision. If you never visualize yourself in health and prosperity, you will never have faith to receive it.

If you can see it, it is yours. Let the eyes of your spirit imagine the Word working in your life. God wants you above and not beneath, as the head and not the tail. (Deut. 28:13.) Let the Word of God perfect that image in your heart.

3. *Keep them in the midst of thine heart.*

The "heart" refers to the spirit man, which is recreated at the new birth. You must continue to feed the Word of God into your spirit. It is not a matter of eating just once. You must continue feeding the Word to maintain a healthy, well-balanced spiritual diet. You must keep it rolling over and over within your heart.

As one man has said, "Many people feed their bodies three hot meals a day, and their spirits one cold snack a week." It is not enough to feed your body once a week. It is likewise not sufficient to feed your spirit once in a while. Your entire man needs food every day.

All successful athletes, both professional and competitive amateurs, must keep themselves in outstanding physical condition. They have controls on the quality and quantity of food that they eat. They have daily programs of exercise to keep their bodies finely tuned. They continually practice, going over and over again, the moves that will be demanded of them to be the best. This is accepted and expected as a part of success in an athlete's life.

Success with the laws of the Spirit come in the same manner. You must control what is fed into your spirit. Feed on the Word that will cause growth in the area you desire. Keep yourself proficient in the Word, putting it into practice in your daily life. Practice will make you perfect.

In Joshua 14:7,8 Caleb describes the key to his success in entering the land God promised Israel:

Forty years old was I when Moses the servant of the Lord sent me from Kadesh-barnea to espy out the land; and I brought him word again as it was in mine heart.

Nevertheless my brethren that went up with me made the heart of the people melt: but I wholly followed the Lord my God.

Because God has said that the land belonged to Israel, Caleb could visualize them living there. Notice that the report he gave was what was alive in his heart. God's Word was alive in him.

However, the evil report came back also. These men had seen the same land, but they were not considering what God had spoken. The evil report *made the heart of the people melt.* Your ears and eyes are the gateways to your heart. This is why we are told in Proverbs 4:23, *Keep thy heart with all diligence; for out of it are the issues of life.*

God's life power flows out of your heart. You must protect your heart from input that is contrary to the Word of God. Caleb protected his heart when their report came. He kept the Word alive within him and later enjoyed the fruit of his faith.

These three areas — the ears, the eyes, and the heart — work together toward the goal of expanding the hope of the believer. When hope is expanded, it gives a greater capacity for faith.

5

Conceiving God's Word

Through meditation the creative ability of God is developed in your heart. The things God wants to do for you must be conceived in your spirit before they become a reality in your life.

Here is an example from the New Testament of how you can give birth to the Word of God in the earth:

And in the sixth month the angel Gabriel was sent from God unto a city of Galilee, named Nazareth, to a virgin espoused to a man whose name was Joseph, of the house of David; and the virgin's name was Mary.

And the angel came in unto her, and said, Hail, thou that art highly favoured, the Lord is with thee: blessed art thou among women.

And when she saw him, she was troubled at his saying, and cast in her mind what manner of salutation this should be.

And the angel said unto her, Fear not, Mary: for thou hast found favour with God. And, behold, thou shalt conceive in thy womb, and bring forth a son, and shalt call his name JESUS. He shall be great, and shall be called the Son of the Highest: and the Lord God shall give unto him the throne of his father David: and he shall reign over the house of Jacob for ever; and of his kingdom there shall be no end.

Then said Mary unto the angel, How shall this be, seeing I know not a man?

And the angel answered and said unto her, The Holy Ghost shall come upon thee, and the power of the Highest shall overshadow thee: therefore also

that holy thing which shall be born of
thee shall be called the Son of God.

Luke 1:26-35

The angel told Mary of an event
that was absolutely impossible. Never
before in history had a woman given
birth to a child that was conceived by
the Holy Spirit.

If you think you are facing impossible situations, consider Mary's. It
had to be accomplished by the Holy
Spirit, or it would not be done at all.

Every time God gives you an assign-
ment, He will require you to make a
step of faith. God is a faith God, and He
requires faith of His people. You're
required to move by faith. Then it
becomes the responsibility of the Holy
Spirit to bring it to pass.

If you have a situation in your life
that looks impossible, God said
something to Mary that you need to
hear. He said, *For with God nothing*

shall be impossible (Luke 1:37). There isn't a situation in your life beyond the realm of possibility with God.

Notice in verse 34 Mary asked the angel a question: *How shall this be, seeing I know not a man?*

The angel had also visited a man named Zacharias and told him he would have a son. To Zacharias this was an impossibility since his wife Elisabeth was barren. Zacharias also asked the angel a question: *Whereby shall I know this?* (v. 18). In other words, "How do I know you are telling the truth?"

From these two examples we learn that it must be permissible to ask a question of an angel. But each question received a different result. Mary's question did not challenge God. She simply wanted to know how it would be done. The answer came: "By the Holy Ghost."

However, Zacharias questioned God's integrity. That is not the way to respond to God, and Zacharias realized this after he was struck speechless.

When God speaks to you, don't look for a sign. God doesn't lead by signs. Believers are not expected to follow signs; signs are to follow believers.

God leads you by your spirit. He will speak to you in your spirit; then if a confirming sign comes by the Holy Spirit, you can receive it with joy.

There are three things the Holy Spirit did concerning Mary which brought God's desire into existence.

First, the Holy Spirit came upon her. Of course, the Holy Spirit dwells within you, but He can also come upon you. The only way the Holy Spirit can fully operate in your life is by your spending time with Him. You must worship Him, commune with Him, and listen to Him.

Intercession is God's hearing your voice and moving on behalf of your words. Meditation is your hearing God's voice and moving on behalf of His words.

Second, the power of the Highest will overshadow you. That is to be an uninterrupted arrangement. Psalm 91:1 instructs us to *abide under the shadow of the Almighty.* Abiding is something that is done all day and all night. Abiding under His influence will enable you to draw from the wisdom of God. When you make decisions, you can be confident that you are following the leadership of your heavenly Father.

Third, Mary conceived and gave birth to the Word of God. When you were born again, the Word of God was planted, or conceived, in your spirit. Much in the same manner, the Word of God was conceived in the womb of Mary. Jesus is the Word made flesh. (John 1:14.)

Therefore, all the miraculous power of God resides within every believer. The problem has been that relatively few have ever given birth to or brought forth the Word that was conceived within them.

You must give birth to the Word which you have conceived. Many times the Word of God, or the seed planted, just lies dormant inside Christians. Consequently, they seldom experience the power of God in answer to their prayers. Ephesians 3:20 gives great insight into this problem: *Now unto him that is able to do exceeding abundantly above all that we ask or think, according to the power that worketh in us . . . .*

Everyone knows God is able to do the miraculous. His ability is not the question. The question is, "How do you get the miraculous to happen for you?" The scripture does not say it is according to the power in you, but it is according to the power that is *alive* and *at work in you!* Once the Word is conceived, you must keep it alive and active in you.

You may better understand this principle by taking a view of its negative counterpart. James 1:14,15 says, *But every man is tempted, when he is drawn away of his own lust, and enticed. Then when lust hath conceived, it bringeth forth sin: and sin, when it is finished, bringeth forth death.*

Lust, or desire, must be conceived before sin results. This reveals the avenue which activates the spiritual laws of death in your life. Sin always puts you in a position where Satan can take advantage of you. Once you sin, the laws of death immediately begin to move in. You lose your peace. Strife and confusion begin to operate. Sin is a destructive force, and its ultimate goal is death.

In Acts 5:4 Peter asks a question of Ananias: *Why hast thou conceived this thing in thine heart? thou hast not lied unto men, but unto God.* Ananias had conceived sin in his heart. The desire for the adulation of men and the greed for money caused deception to be planted in his heart. Once it had been planted, or conceived, it brought forth fruit, which was death. Many people wonder who killed Ananias and Sapphira — God or Satan. Actually, sin killed them. According to James, they were drawn away of their *own lust,* and sin brought forth death.

Let's view this progression referred to by James with a positive viewpoint. *When the desire of God is conceived, it brings forth faith; and faith, when it is finished, brings forth life.*

The life of God can flow through you and bring forth the good and perfect gifts from God, but it is your responsibility to give birth to them once they have been conceived in your heart. The life force is available. Every need you have can be met. Every impossible situation can be solved. The answers will come as you meditate in the Word of God and allow His desires to become your desires, then give birth to them.

6
Expanding Your Capacity For Faith

For whatsoever things were written aforetime were written for our learning, that we through patience and comfort of the scriptures might have hope.

Romans 15:4

One of the goals or purposes of the Scriptures in your life is to develop and increase your hope. God is a God of hope and He wants your hope to greatly abound.

Now the God of hope fill you with all joy and peace in believing, that ye may abound in hope, through the power of the Holy Ghost.

Romans 15:13

Many times hope is a neglected part of the Christian life. Hope alone will never bring results from God's Word. But when hope is developed in the Word of God, then used in connection with faith, you will begin to see the move of God in your life as you have desired.

Too often in an effort to make faith work, people have overlooked the necessity of hope in God's Word. But as you study the Bible, you will find that hope is an extremely important part of success with God.

Hebrews 11:1 says, *Now faith is the substance of things hoped for, the evidence of things not seen.* What can faith give substance to if there is no hope? You must have hope in God's Word before your faith can produce anything.

Hope sets the goal for your faith. Once the goal is set, your faith can go into operation to bring that goal from

God's Word into the present physical world.

Meditating in the Word of God brings these hopes and goals into clear view. The goals God has for you become more vivid each day. As your hope is expanded, your capacity for faith is also expanded. When you put faith into operation, you have a clear picture of what your faith is bringing to pass.

This is the same principle God used in creation. He had an inner picture of what He expected the universe to look like. He knew what He expected man to look like. He had a hope, or a goal, and He released faith with His words which created the images He had within Him.

Hope is a confident and favorable expectation. When you allow the Word to create a favorable expectation, then add your faith to that expectation, you have a winning combination.

This helps to explain why many people fail to receive healing in their bodies, even though they believe in the principles of faith and healing. Some have even died. Somewhere along the way, they lose their hope. They lose sight of their "confident and favorable expectation." They become hopeless. They don't see themselves getting well. They don't see themselves getting out of bed. They have lost all hope of being healed. Their goal is no longer to continue the fight of faith, but to simply go on to be with Jesus.

There is no prayer of faith that will change that. There is little anyone can do for a person who has laid down his hope for receiving from God.

Proverbs 13:12 says, *Hope deferred maketh the heart sick.* Unless you make the effort to keep your hope and expectation in God's Word, you will become sick and weak in your heart. It is vitally important to have a strong and active hope.

Abraham received a hope from God that he would have a son. To Abraham's mind, all hope was gone of having a son, but the Bible says of him: *Who against hope believed in hope . . .* (Rom. 4:18).

Against natural hope, Abraham chose to believe the hope God set before him. It was supernatural hope — a goal that could not be accomplished without a miracle from God. He applied his faith to the hope from God, and the result was a son.

When God told Abraham to take his son and offer him as a burnt sacrifice, Abraham instantly began to form a picture in his spirit. He saw himself taking Isaac to the mountain, slaying him, and offering him as a sacrifice. Isaac was as good as dead, because Abraham had determined to obey God's command.

At the same time, however, Abraham knew the promise God had

given concerning Isaac. God's Word had produced hope. Isaac was to be the seed from which an entire nation would be born. That promise had to be fulfilled; therefore, Isaac would have to be raised from the dead.

Abraham told the men to wait for them at the foot of the mountain. He said, *I and the lad will go yonder and worship, and come again to you* (Gen. 22:5). He was confident that both of them were going to return.

Abraham had the image alive in him of God raising up Isaac. *By faith Abraham, when he was tried, offered up Isaac . . . Accounting that God was able to raise him up, even from the dead; from whence also he received him in a figure* (Heb. 11:17-19). What Abraham accounted that God would do was his hope. Because of that hope, he could respond in faith toward God.

Active hope that is established in God's Word will bring stability to your soul — your mind, reasoning, and emotions. Hebrews 6:19 calls hope "an anchor of the soul."

Having a clear image in your spirit of God's desire for you will keep your soul from drifting off the Word. It will keep you single-minded. You will not toy with ideas that contradict the hope that is within you. When something comes to convince you that the Word will not work this time, your spirit will be *alive with hope* in God's Word. Hope will keep sending scriptural evidence to reinforce your mind and keep you sure and steadfast in the Word of God.

7
Drawing Out Wisdom

Happy is the man that findeth wisdom.

Proverbs 3:13

The wisdom of God is one of the most precious commodities in existence. Wisdom is what gives you the ability to properly apply the knowledge you attain in God's Word. This is what makes it so valuable. The Bible teaches that it is of more value than gold or rubies. *Wisdom is the principal thing; therefore get wisdom: and with all thy getting get understanding* (Prov. 4:7).

Where does wisdom come from? How do you acquire it? Proverbs 2:6,7 explains: *For the Lord giveth wisdom:*

out of his mouth cometh knowledge and understanding. He layeth up sound wisdom for the righteous: he is a buckler to them that walk uprightly.

Wisdom comes out of God's mouth. The words that come out His mouth are given to us in the Bible. This is God's wisdom and it is available to all believers.

Do you want to cultivate wisdom? It comes by meditation in the Word. As you meditate in God's Word, it becomes a part of you; therefore, God's wisdom becomes a part of you. It becomes your wisdom. Your way will become prosperous and you will act wisely.

Notice again Proverbs 3:13: *Happy is the man that findeth wisdom.* If wisdom must be found, then we can assume that it is hidden. But the Word also says it is laid up *for* you, not from you. There is a big difference.

Wisdom is hidden *from* the world and laid up *for* His family. But God's wisdom must be sought after. You must dig for it. Like the wise man who built his house upon a rock (Luke 6:48), you must dig deep to find the hidden wisdom of God.

How do you get wisdom? *Receive my words, and hide my commandments with thee; so that thou incline thine ear unto wisdom, and apply thine heart to understanding; Yea, if thou criest after knowledge, and liftest up thy voice for understanding; if thou seekest her as silver, and searchest for her as for hid treasures; then shalt thou understand the fear of the Lord, and find the knowledge of God* (Prov. 2:1-5).

You must first *find* God's wisdom. All of the treasures of wisdom are in Christ, and Christ is in you. Draw it out of the Word through meditation. Let His Word teach, guide, and dwell in you richly. When you become God-inside-minded, you will become wisdom-minded.

 **Dennis Burke** has affected thousands of people through a refreshing approach to God's Word and the power of the Holy Spirit. The demand upon Dennis' ministry takes him to a different part of the United States every week and also into Canada, Australia, and the United Kingdom.

Dennis began as an associate pastor and youth minister in Southern California. There he obtained tremendous insight into the work of the local church. Following this, he and his wife Vikki moved to Fort Worth, Texas, to work with Kenneth Copeland. After Dennis had traveled with the Copeland ministry for two years, God led him to enter his own ministry in 1979.

The simplicity and balance with which Dennis teaches brings powerful insight for successful Christian living.

For a complete list of tapes and books by
Dennis Burke, or to receive his publication,
Words to the Wise, write:

Dennis Burke Ministries
P.O. Box 793
Arlington, TX 76010

*Feel free to include your prayer requests and
comments when you write.*

How To Meditate God's Word
is available at your local bookstore.

Harrison House • P. O. Box 35035 • Tulsa, OK 74153